3 o'clock in the

meantime

Victoria Halley Osland

Presentation by *BookLeaf Publishing*

Web: www.bookleafpub.com

E-mail: info@bookleafpub.com

ISBN: 978-93-95890-49-6

First edition 2022

religion is the only language we've been given in which to speak about forgiveness

forgive me i haven't told the story
just expected you to understand or rather
hoped that when you'd pressed your palms
together
and leaned your cheek for sleep
you were saying a prayer for forever
the deep and haunted type of forever

forgive me i haven't provided the context
just expected you to read
the shake of my head when i declined
your invitation to sleep
just sleep, innocent sleep, you said
you meant chaste sleep
which seemed hollow considering
the openness which which
i'd introduced myself to you

forgive me i thought you knew what i meant
when i said i don't let people care for me
i thought you'd choke on saying
come here and let me take care of it

forgive me i would've let you

shower me in

we used to do gin shots on a weeknight and i'd
ask you to join me in the shower
you'd decline, stating you'd showered that
morning or the night before,
you'd laugh because most people showered
every day but we didn't
i'd steam the bathroom and prune my skin
shed my hair and gather it in tangles over my
fingers like i was wearing hair gloves
even after declining to join me you'd open the
unlocked door to the roar of the downpour
hitting the porcelain tub
my hands at my ears scrubbing my scalp with
the pads of my fingers
you'd smile at me in this big goofy way
toothily some would say
toothily i would say
giddy from the gin you'd laugh and slide open
the curtain
why can't i leave you alone? you'd ask
lips exposing your crooked front teeth
i'd laugh
say i don't know baby and swirl around to face
the water

close my eyes and put my whole face in the
stream
ears dripping i'd turn back to you
put both sopping hands on your cheeks and kiss
your mouth
using the back of your hand you'd wipe the
water from your face
and i'd love you so much

la petite morte

i think there's something wrong with me but i
hate when people say there's something wrong
with them
i hate how vicious my boyfriend is in bed
i keep listening to that song from burlesque, a
guy what takes his time
and i wish he would slow down and make me
feel adored again
i watch porn now and i never did before
always lesbian porn
and all it takes to make me cum is an up-close
shot
of a swollen pussy
or full and perky tits
or a diamond butt plug sliding smoothly into a
hot girl's ass
and yeah sometimes i think about my boyfriend
while i fuck myself with my penguin pleasurer
but not always and mostly i think about a hot
girl pushing my face onto his dick
i googled low sperm count today because my
boyfriend says he comes inside me but i never
see the mess
lexapro can decrease sperm count
age can decrease sperm count

lower sperm count can make it harder to have
children
my boyfriend is eight years older than me
when i ask him to go slow and tender he acts
like i am boring him
i finally know how to cum
it's been a long time coming
(i'm not past a good joke)
but the point i'm trying to make is that i know
what pleasure feels like now
and i'm looking for it everywhere i go
in that way i think i am like a fifteen-year-old
boy
i didn't grow up touching myself
i grew up pushing other people's hands away
i think i would offend my boyfriend if i asked
him to have a threesome with me
i probably wouldn't even like it
i don't like to share

we are a syllable

the edges and parameters and endings and
beginnings didn't actually matter, as long as we
had a strong centre

drunken fluency

i grabbed his arm and pulled him into the
parking lot where i'd parked my red honda. he
tripped over his left foot before catching his
balance and following my direction.
"is canadian tire still open?" he asked.
i pulled my phone out and started googling.
canadian tire hours.
"probably not. Iit's a quarter after ten. why do
you need to go to canadian tire?"
he stopped walking and gritted his teeth before
speaking. "i need to buy you a knife."
"why?"
he gestured around him, downtown kitchener
revealed in the flourish of his tattooed arm. "it's
not safe for you to be walking around here
alone."
i took a deep breath. "i don't need a knife."
he grabbed my hand. "are you sure?"
"yep."
he continued staring at me. "downtown is
sketchy. You never know…"
"i don't need a knife," i repeated.
"i'll buy you a knife."
"get in the car."

rosy full moon

you said it feels like you've been writing letters
to me, so i thought i'd sit down and really write
you one, where i tell you that you're my ideal
reader. that part of stephen king's book really
resonated with me—the part where you're really
just writing for one specific person, hoping
they'll understand you. i don't know why i want
you to know me so much. we don't even know
each other. something drew me to you when i
heard you read for the first time. we were in 303
with dr. bouvier. your story was about coke, and
i have a bad habit of adopting the struggles of
the people i love.

my closest friend spent a year addicted to coke.
we were seventeen years old, spending high
school lunches in her tiny pontiac vibe, going
through the tim horton's drive through with
cigarettes in our hands. blue next, or belmont
when we could afford them. we were always
getting laid off from or calling in to our grocery
store jobs.

her boyfriend was rich though. or I guess his
parents were. lived in the fancy neighbourhood
in town, not that you'd know it by name. i'm
sure you could guess what it looked like though.

i'm still not sure how many bedrooms it had, but i had my own bedroom there for when i stayed over after house parties. the entire basement was bigger than my whole house. we drank shitty beer and went skinny dipping in the pond in the backyard when i was in high school.

he was older than we were, by three years, which matters when you're in the eighth grade, which is how old em was when she and lincoln started dating. They were together almost five years. an impressive feat, a year longer than my own high school relationship.

lincoln bought our cigarettes.

when I first started smoking, i wanted menthols, green next. you can't get those anymore unless you go to the hasty market on gage, past seven p.m., and paid with cash. dante and i used to do that. he'd walk up westmount from his uptown apartment (he didn't have a car or a driver's license, a sore spot for me) and surprise me with the menthols i loved. we'd drink too much in the bar under his apartment. it was straight out of a sitcom, some how i met your mother shit, but the irony is that dante didn't want to get married or have kids. can't be a mother with no children, can you, vic?

you can baby your boyfriends all you want, vic, but that doesn't make you a mother. i wanted dante to get his license. i started teaching him how to drive, but then i slept with someone else, so we stopped driving together. he doesn't know. i've told a couple people. drinking lets me speak too freely, and i so desperately want to be understood that i'll choke over my own words just to leave some kind of impression. and now I'm telling you. i hope you won't think of me differently. i don't know if you think of me at all. if you have a perception of the girl in your editing group with a drinking problem and a pathological need to explain herself. if it's a particularly positive impression. i bet it's not, but i bet i deserve it.

or maybe i'm just being mean to myself again, i tend to do that. i tend to project my own disappointment in myself onto other people and then get mad at them for the way i think they see me.

i did it to my mom a couple months ago. i got a dog five years, almost exactly, because i was turning seventeen. god, i was seventeen five years ago. what the fuck is that, huh?

we were living in a townhouse, much too small for the five of us, but it was the first place we ever lived that my dad couldn't make shudder with thrown dishes or threats or jumping up and down screaming that we were all disappointing him. my mom didn't have a bedroom. she slept in the living room, on a pullout couch for two

years before we moved into the house we're in
now.

i was depressed and half insane, and i wanted a
dog to get me up in the morning and out in the
evening. i saved the money I made from sobeys,
or at least whatever i didn't spend on cigarettes
and books, and found a breeder in wellington
county. i bought a dog that didn't shed and
wouldn't get too big. i named him kota.

god, this is all so boring. i'm trying to entertain
myself with the happenings of my own life, and
i have no interest. i'm sorry for wasting your
time.

you'll hate this loyalty until you need it

one day you will be grateful for the forgiveness
and loyalty i have in me
one day you will be on the receiving end of this
grace and you will not begrudge me of it
eventually i will hold you softly in a place
reserved for past lovers and the people I used to
be, and you will be thankful i maintain the space
for those people because one day you will be
one of them

haiku

another springtime
blooms same as the last and the
old hurt never dies

i am perfect for
those grown men whose lives never
caught up with their years

folding into the
arms of men who couldn't love
me and never tried

there is darkness here
between the folds of your ribs
human and broken

i flaunt my heart in
a life fight, caught with a gun
between you and me

what is a peacock
but the engorged clit of a
fuckable woman

if you've never been

licked within an inch of your
short meaningless life

chances are you're too
open for the chasm of
my experience

my storied life holds
the worst and heaviest glass
of frozen water

my mother cringes
when she hears me chewing ice
"suck on something else"

i would melt the fruit
of desire between my lips
if i could swallow

the difference between
holding right and squeezing too
tight is the distance

i'm too open for
my own good and you'd rather
i remain that way

like love at a hate
crime, like the sun at a

tidal wave storm fight

like a kid at a
divorce hearing, like goodbye
at a door closing

like a doorbell at
i want you to come over
without even calling

like proposing at
i'm too young to have dealt with
any of this shit

like just sobbing at
i'll hold you but i won't be
happy about it

old poem about an old friend

my hands ache from
smoothing your hard corners
from telling your voice to soften
from telling your hands to ease up.
i've got burn marks from your tongue
a hand print on my ass
and i have let you mark me
with your growing
it makes me ache for the next girl
who finds you smooth and gentle
for whom you'll ask
and then ask again, "are you sure"
the one who will know
your unshared attention
perhaps know you better
than i ever did
it makes me ache for the next girl
to whom you will not mention me
except briefly as an old friend
but you are not an old friend to me

retirement living

it was an enduringly hot summer, one where you
wished the air conditioning in the retirement
home was a lot harsher than the old folks could
stand. And yet, you were just a guest there,
someone who came into their home to serve
them their meals and go. you could keep your
own house as cool as you'd like, and yet you
spent more waking hours in theirs than your
own.

        if we're ever reduced to used to be, just
know i'll keep it all, irreparably woven and
irretrievably hidden in who i have become.

he doesn't begrudge me my past and
understands that i am who i am because of it.

in the name of everything you've ever dropped,
'til death to we forever and ever, and ever again,
amen.

this is me performing femininity; this is me just
short of myself.

i used to smoke cigarettes
before eating because i
enjoyed feeling empty

i only ever want
in the instance of loss
to have screamed fuck you

i am only myself
in perennial torment

lonely

i've been lonely lately and i don't want to make
it anyone else's responsibility but i notice that
because of this loneliness i'm a little harder to be
around. i talk mostly about myself and get
impatient when people take too long to say
things, or when they repeat themselves, or tell
me something i already know. weird how this is
some kind of menacing circle — i become
lonely, i inadvertently push people away, and
that makes me more lonely. i always say i'm an
introvert and that i enjoy my own company, and
while this is true, part of being an introvert is my
desperate need to be understood combined with
my selectiveness when choosing company. this
is what makes is so hard when my chosen
company is unavailable. em and mila don't live
in the city and i miss having them around. i feel
like i don't ask em about her life in san francisco
enough. mila has so many friends in toronto and
talking to her sometimes makes me feel small.
ali and i are drifting because as disgusting as the
notion is, she triggers me. i hate saying it like
that. but i can't talk about, think about, know
anything specific about her boyfriend because it
sets my skin on fire. i get jealous that she can be

so loud about her brokenness and claim it as an identity. even today, she said that if she ever got pregnant, she'd come to me and make me choose whether she kept the child or not. i had a pregnancy scare last week, and it made me want to curl up and die. i didn't tell her or my mom about it. am i lonely or am i isolating myself? i bought a pregnancy test. it cost me twenty dollars, which i definitely couldn't afford but i couldn't ask for help paying for it because that would mean someone would know. and i'm tired of being a financial burden. i thought about if the test came back positive, what would i do. i'd end up calling dr. fuss and quietly and heartbreakingly booking my own abortion appointment. i thought about not even telling dante. i thought about how i couldn't tell mom because she doesn't believe in abortion. but i couldn't give a baby a life and i knew if i had the baby and gave it up, i would have confetti for a heart. i can't do that so soon after bailey. and for some reason i just feel like i have to do all of this alone. and then i resent people for not knowing that i am Doing This Alone.

i had a dream that dante had a dream about bailey and it inspired him to go get him back for me. i wish he understood how devastating this is for me. to lose bailey. every relationship i've had has ended like, "oh so you're really not done

hurting me yet? no? not yet" and it is killing me.
i listen to that fiona song all the time where she's
like, i might be so sick in the head i need to be
bled dry to quit, or maybe i just really used to
love him, i hope that's it.
god i hope that's it.
the parts of my life have never looked the way i
thought they would. i think about my halloween
party and how happy i was to be surrounded by
all my people. and they were all there too —
except mila. em, richard, robynne, amine,
khalid, jordan, ali, erica, mom, alex, katie, drew,
dante. it was perfect, it really was. i use it to
remind myself i am loved. even when those
people live in san francisco, toronto, guelph; are
busy doing school and with their stupid
boyfriends and play dungeons and dragons;
unfortunately in unrequited love with me or
think of me as a sex object; and say the same
things over and over again.

echoes

when they say fucking someone is like fucking
everyone they've ever fucked, it's meant to be a
shame tool. i find it true but not shameful, true
as me living in the past, true as me invested in
my own roots, true as the palimpsest i have
made myself at home in.

when i hold your cock in my hands and think
about the tip hitting the back of my throat, how
can i not think about the time i got fucked in the
face so hard i threw up, ran to the bathroom to
spit out my puke, and returned my throat to the
dick it belonged to.

and when that guy asked me, vic what are you
even into? what, has no one ever asked you that
before? i'm so sorry to hear, you must not have
been having very good sex

and i'd exclaim, listen i dated everyone else i
have ever fucked,

and he'd croon, vic, oh vic honey, why did you
do that?

and i'd tentatively say, suggest things and i'll tell
you if they're okay or not

and he'd say, no that's a cop-out

and i'd want to say, that's the only way i know
how to talk about sex, i only know how to say
yes or no, and even then,
and he'd ask me, choking?
and i'd say yes
and he'd ask, ass-slapping?
and i'd say yes,
and he'd say, how hard? like that? with a whack
and i'd say harder,
and he'd smack me harder, the spit of his hand
against my ass, like a frying pan just taken off
the stove and hit with water
and my eyes would water as i tried to laugh it
off, that's a little too hard
and just as bodies can easily remind us of other
bodies,
i'm brought back to when i had been punished in
this way
not "punished" but punished, the real stuff
akin to "i would have hate-fucked you but i was
too disgusted by your behaviour"
because again, i laughed it off
we laugh off our pain as if it doesn't exist unless
you press on it
but baby most pain doesn't look like bruises
it burns all on its own
this whole time we've been trying to write
poetry with a shotgun

when all i've ever wanted was to be loved in the
language of love
and nothing more

body

i've been thinking a lot about how bodies hold
memory. a lot of that memory exists in sexual
triggers — one body's thrust may feel like
another body's embrace. i imagine coming back
together with him after over a year, of my body
explaining, this is all that i've endured since we
were last together. since the last time you held
me like this, licked me like this, these are the
ways my body has been handled.

and when dante holds me after sex, his cock still
inside me as he lays on top of me, resting his
head on my collarbone, he notices the scar on
my neck. thin, faint, white line vertical down the
middle of my neck.
"do you have a scar on your neck?" he asks.
i smile forlornly. "yeah, i do."
"what's that from?"
i feel like i'm chewing my bottom lip, looking
for the right words. "bailey," is what i end up
saying.
"dog?" he asks.
i confirm, yes, bailey was the dog i got with my
ex when we lived together. i stopped speaking to
my ex for a month or two, even though we still

shared this dog, and in that time he gave bailey
back to the people we got him from, over a year
after the fact.
and the scar on my neck will always remind me
that not even a lovely little mutt named bailey
could've survived the split.

bedtime

like two twin beds shoved up against each other
to appear as one
or maybe like a queen size bed split down the
middle by a body pillow
or the two of us in one bed with our own sets of
twin blankets
together but apart

preacher's twitter

sing me a lullaby, will you?
the one about the stars and how you wouldn't
know how to find me in them
you make basements out of the girls you love
like you know you'll be the tornado
i'm just the girl in the shower singing songs
you've never even heard of
songs you doesn't know the words to
love songs
we could've been soft for the rest of our lives
but i know
i know you don't want to know what keeps me
up at night
unless it's you
maybe you wouldn't know but i've always had
my eyes open
you could've been a crack in the sidewalk too
stop looking for love down her annoying throat
i'm right here you fucking piece of shit
no, don't say you're sorry
cut her tongue out of her mouth
the way you can't write about christmas without
writing about snow
you can't write about love without writing about
me

a girl named worship,
a boy on his knees
i wish i'd known to tell you
girls like me don't last long
(you can catch cynicism like mono)
took the bus home to where i used to love
used to live
it's all the same
what i mean to say is,
lick up my melting heart and tell me how it
tastes,
my real name is baby
i want to live forever in the night we first met
i wish we could last as long as i do
sometimes i want to eat everything that doesn't
remind you of me
i am a heart entirely too big for the chest it was
born in
love is when putting someone first
doesn't make them think that you come second
i've always been better than church
i feel like i tried crawling into your lap
and you just told me i wasn't a lap dog
or a love dog or something like that
i have a heart murmur but it just talks about you
breaking a clean heart in half means
you'll only ever get censored love back
i hope a night of loveless love
reminds you i made you feel good

i dream of you so softly
i don't even remember when i wake up
i can love the hardest parts of you
but i can't make you soft
some days i'm sure i'm made entirely of mercy
you were like, would you mind being the love of
my life?
and i was like, have you even been listening?
there's a part of me lost
in the bruise on your neck
heaven is just where people fall in love
and stay that way
i feel like a high-five that just wants to be held
i used to think if i asked god for light
he'd just send me you
look i've made my heart walls so fucking thin
and you're still not listening
my favourite sex position is the one where
you come over without calling
the currency for getting into heaven
is how many people you could've hurt
but didn't
it's just that some people are so scared
to get sick of their favourite song
that they never even listen to it and
some people love that way too
you tell your new lover you have a bruise
and they push on the way i used to
forgive you out loud

you'll never convince a poet
to use her inside voice
my hands hurt when i think about the versions of
you i haven't touched
more beautiful girls have touched you
more fascinating girls have offered their hearts
as temporary residence
i am a crack in the sidewalk
and you have your eyes wide open
the last poem we share will be a passing glance
if the stars will bear witness
we were tied together with strings around our
fingers
in place of wedding rings
'til death do us forever and ever
all over again amen

i used to miss my past lovers

french has no word for sick
instead we are
bad in the head
bad in the heart
i am mal à la tête mama
mama i am mal à la coeur
mama my heart hurts
i have a bad heart mama
j'ai mal à la
vie mama
i'm sick in my life mama
i'm sick to death of everything that
has ever happened to me
j'ai mal à la
life mama
mal par everything that
has ever happened
french has no word for home mama
in french i miss you
means you are missing from me
but i need a language where
i miss you means
how long until my body
stops asking where you are

if i were my own lover, this is how i would describe myself

she had a steel ball on her tongue that moved
when she talked and clicked against her teeth
when she told me her name. her hair looked like
it didn't quite know how to fall. somewhere
between wavy and straight, it fell in a curtain
over her forehead, and she routinely pushed it
out of the way.

Printed in the USA
CPSIA information can be obtained
at www.ICGtesting.com
LVHW011539050124
767941LV00091B/5138